Washington
Bookplates

Also from Westphalia Press
westphaliapress.org

Washington Bookplates

Six Articles Reprinted from
The Town Crier, 1925-1926

---

by
Frederick Starr

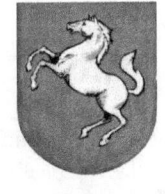

WESTPHALIA PRESS
An Imprint of Policy Studies Organization

Washington Bookplates: Six Articles Reprinted from *The Town Crier*, 1925-1926
All Rights Reserved © 2017 by Policy Studies Organization

Westphalia Press
An imprint of Policy Studies Organization
1527 New Hampshire Ave., NW
Washington, D.C. 20036
info@ipsonet.org

ISBN-13: 978-1-63391-535-0
ISBN-10: 1-63391-535-2

Cover design by Jeffrey Barnes:
jbarnesbook.design

Daniel Gutierrez-Sandoval, Executive Director
PSO and Westphalia Press

Updated material and comments on this edition
can be found at the Westphalia Press website:
www.westphaliapress.org

WASHINGTON BOOKPLATES

BY
FREDERICK STARR

Six Articles reprinted from
THE TOWN CRIER
1925-26

SEATTLE
1927

WASHINGTON BOOKPLATES

H AVING been interested in bookplates (ex-libris) elsewhere, and especially in their local development and in the personality of their artists, it was natural that in settling down in a new home I should inquire as to their development and use here, in the State of Washington. It would have been no great surprise if none, or but a few, had been encountered. Our state is new; our people have been busy with the every-day rush of making and developing a commonwealth. Is it reasonable to expect to find here any considerable indulgence in the use of a trifling elegance, such as a bookplate? However, more have already been discovered than were anticipated and the list of those who own and use a bookplate in this state must be a long one.

* * *

What constitutes a "Washington bookplate?" What shall we include in our list? (a) We must count all bookplates owned and used by persons living in our state, wherever they were made, by whomsoever, and at whatever time. Even if a bookplate were made for Smith of Philadelphia, by a New York artist, if Smith now lives in Seattle (or anywhere in Washington) it must be credited to us. Use by a Washingtonian will qualify. (b) We shall, of course, count as Washington bookplates all that were made by Washington artists, for people living elsewhere. We shall claim all credit of design and execution by home talent. (c) The most characteristically Washington bookplates are such as are made by Washington artists for persons living in the state.

* * *

In the hope of arousing a wider interest in the subject, of encouraging the possession and use of a bookplate, and of making a census of Washington bookplates, we plan a short series of articles on the subject. We desire to call attention to bookplates of exceptional interest; to describe some that are notable for the personality of the owner, or for their significance and fitness, or for artistic merit; to make known the work of Washington artists. We beg the assistance of readers. We wish to print a list of all Washington bookplates. Please send in your name and a specimen of your plate, if you own one. If you do not own one, but know friends who do and whose names are not in our list, please send them in. If you are a collector of bookplates, or know of collectors in the state, let us know. There must be some hundreds of Washington bookplates. We know, as yet, only about fifty — almost confined to Seattle and Spokane.

* * *

There is a bookplate world. Hundreds of pamphlets and books have been written about these little marks of book-ownership. There are collectors of bookplates—thousands of them— and collections run to enormous numbers. No doubt the largest in the world is that of the

British Museum, which contains hundreds of thousands of examples. There are societies for ex-libris study. There are exhibitions from time to time. The American Bookplate Society holds an exhibition annually, which is confined to artists and limited to the showing of their own designs for the year. This exhibition is competitive and awards are made by a committee appointed by the society. This exhibition is shown first at New York and then goes from one to another of the more important cities of the United States, among them Spokane. It has been shown once or twice at Seattle; at most of the cities it is an annual event.

* * *

Braungart, in one of the latest books on ex-libris, introduces the term "gebrauchs-ex-libris," to indicate a bookplate that was really intended to be pasted in books as an owner's mark and not merely made as a work of art or to figure in collections. He calls bookplates that are merely for display, or to tickle the vanity or gratify the pride of the owner, "collection-ex-libris." In a bookplate intended for actual use, he insists that the decorative element should be held in suspense, that the design should be single, simple and appropriate, that the owner's name should appear in full and that the intent of the plate as an owner's mark should be immediately evident. He recognizes that simplification may be carried to an extreme, which lacks art value and leaves uncertainty as to the owner. He would avoid initials or the concealment of the owner's name by any ingenious device. For him there are, then, three types—collector-ex-libris, use-ex-libris, oversimplified uncertain ex-libris.

* * *

Most of the Washington bookplates that we have seen would suit Braungart. They are true use-ex-libris, within the limits of sanity and propriety. They are sufficiently decorative, without their significance being lost in a mass of beautiful but unimportant detail. A bookplate is at its best when it is artistic, when its design is a single idea well worked out, when the design has clear reference to the interest or hobby of the owner, when the name appears in full in lettering that is beautiful and well fitted to the space available. The decorative elements should not be so delicate and detailed as to demand too much study or to detract from the central thought or the main idea of the plate.

* * *

Book-lovers are apt to specialize in local interest. This is particularly true in our Northwest and the number of collectors of works regarding the Oregon Territory, Early Washington and the Far West is already large, and is steadily increasing. An early collector in this field was the late Thomas W. Prosch. He had a bookplate which was suggestive of his occupations and his avocations. The design was a printing press; the side elements recall the early west. The inscription runs: From the Library of Thomas W. Prosch. A curious fact in regard to Mr. Prosch's plate was that he regularly

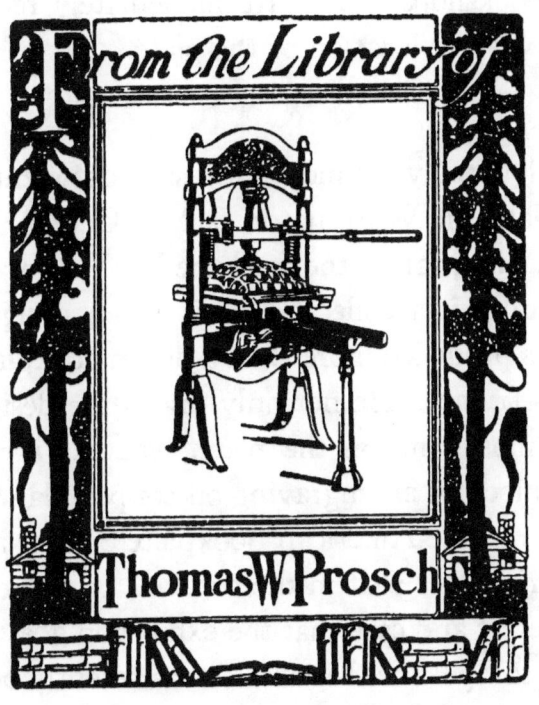

Thomas W. Prosch's Bookplate

pasted it on the inside of the back cover of his books. It is an almost universal custom to place it inside the front cover. One may occasionally find books that belonged to him in the second-hand bookshops. They are immediately recognizable by the location of the plate.

* * *

Undoubtedly the most enthusiastic student of bookplates in Washington is Mr. George W. Fuller, Librarian of the Spokane Public Library. Mr. Fuller is a collector; he is also a designer and has produced more than a dozen bookplates for his friends. He not only draws the designs —he himself makes the plate, whether it is a wood block or an engraving on copper. He is a member of the American Bookplate Society and regularly takes part in the exhibit. It is due to his interest and care that the exhibition goes annually to Spokane. Mr. Fuller has recently been working at a bibliography of ex-libris. There have already been several lists of the books and articles treating of the subject, but his list will come fully up to date and is a thorough and careful piece of work. It is to be printed by the Spokane Public Library and will be of high value to students. At the exhibition of last year,

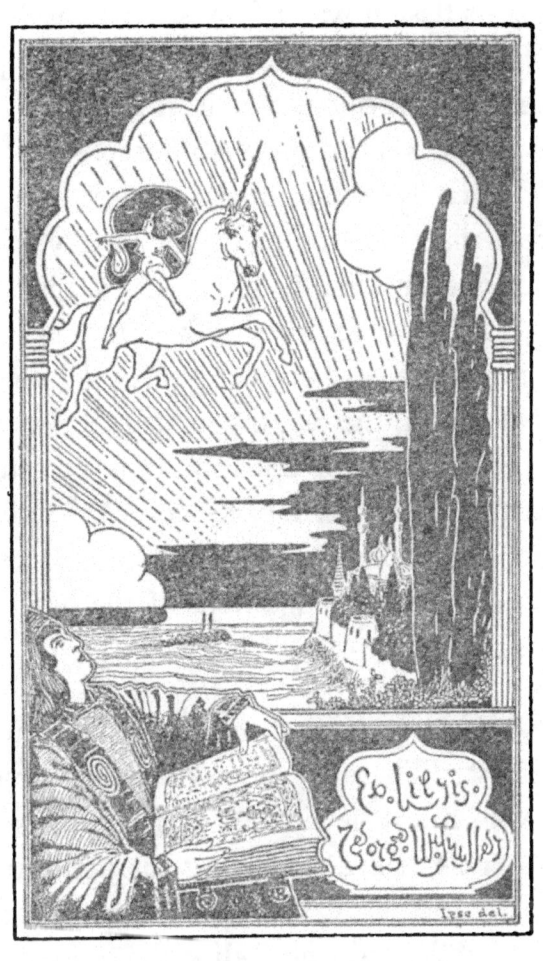

*George W. Fuller's Bookplate
from his own design.*

Mr. Fuller's design was a fantastic witches' caldron. The work on it is so detailed and complicated that a reproduction of it in less than full size would be a failure. As a sample of Mr. Fuller's work—not our own favorite—we reproduce a plate that he made for his own use. A reader is examining a marvel of Arabic calligraphy; as he raises his eyes from the book he catches a glimpse of the vision—the splendor of the sky at sunset, the sea, the walled city on the strait, the horseman of the apocalypse; the tablet bears the words, Ex-Libris George W. Fuller, in letters meant to resemble Arabic characters, in keeping with the suggestions of the design.

II

ESIGNERS of bookplates are three. First: There is the professional artist, who has little time or patience for such artistic trifles, confining his activity to the greater and more impressive art efforts. Once in a while, with the feeling that he is coming down a peg, such an one will "do a plate" for a friend. Yet Albrecht Durer made book-plates—some fine ones. Second: There is the professional designer, who is quite willing to make of bookplates a regular and encouraged part of his work. Most of the best and truly satisfactory bookplates are his work. He special-izes in what Braungart called gebrauchs-ex-li-bris. He may really devote his attention to book-plates and gain national, or even international, reputation in his field. Third: There is the man, who is not a professional artist, who earns his living, if he must earn, in some other field, but who has taste and skill in handling the pen, the brush or the graver, and works in art for the sheer love of it. He makes designs for friends and acquaintances. He often refuses all pecu-niary return. To him some of the most attrac-tive, appropriate and significant bookplates are due. All three of these types of designers are represented among the Seattle bookplate artists. To some of these local producers and their work, this article is devoted.

* * *

Prof. Ambrose Patterson, teacher of painting in the School of Art at the University of Washington, has designed but two bookplates—one for Cecil Brand, officer in the United States Army, now deceased; the other for Mrs. Glenn Hughes.

* * *

The design in Mrs. Hughes' plate is Pierrot reaching towards the moon. Representative of that long line of clowns-fools-buffoons that reaches back from the present to the dramatic renderings of Ancient Greece, "he is a symbol of paradox, suggesting at once naivete and wisdom, fancy and gluttony, joy and sorrow. That is why the mask is in his hand; to present the two complementary moods, which constantly possess him. Night and the moon suggest mystery of art as opposed to the less romantic mystery of sunlight and life. Pierrot is represented as reaching towards the moon, but in his hand he holds a more rational mask which laughs at the moon." As regards the mask—did Mr. Patterson intend it for a portrait? We believe so.

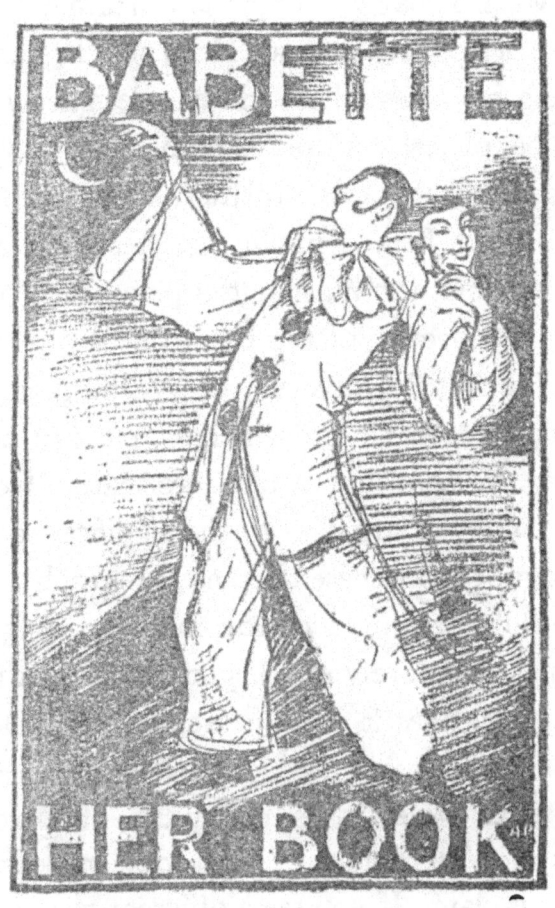

Plate of Mrs. Glenn Hughes
By Ambrose Patterson

Mr. Mark Tobey was with the Cornish School as a teacher of art last year. He is now in Paris, pursuing his art studies. He has designed but three bookplates, two for Washingtonians. We understand that the bookplate he designed for Mrs. Burton James has not as yet been engraved. His other Washington plate, for Prof. Albert R. Lovejoy, of the Department of Dramatic Art at the University of Washington, is here reproduced. It is a remarkable piece of pen drawing. We have no certain information from either owner or artist as to the significance of the design. Under these circumstances each may well indulge his own fancy in discovering a meaning. It is surely not Siegfried and the dragon Fafner; does it come nearer to being Don Quixote and Rosinante? Perhaps it conceals a lesson of struggle against difficulties, of success in the face of obstacles. We shall make no strenuous claim. If you see a different meaning, you are welcome to your opinion. We have done our part in introducing the plate to you.

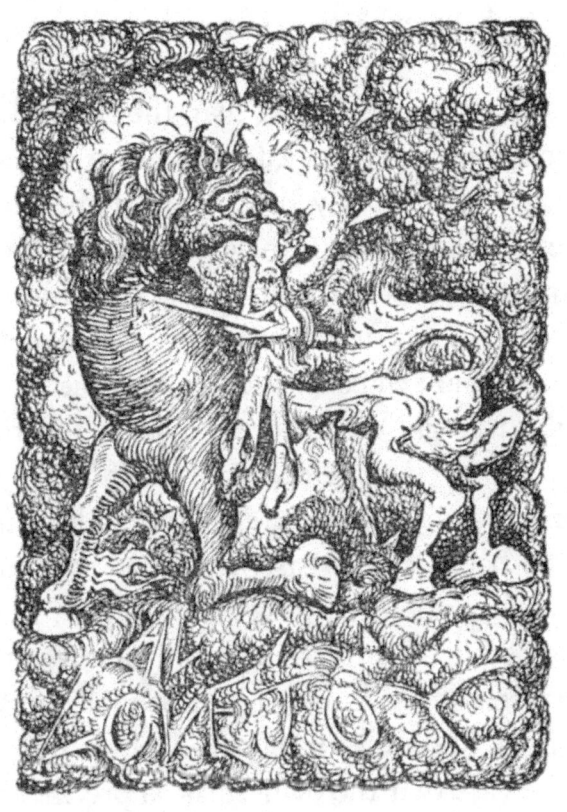

Albert R. Lovejoy's Plate
By Mark Tobey

We believe that other striking and interesting designs may be expected from the same artist.

* * *

It is the exception, rather than the rule, when the bookplate artist has a free hand in making the design. Commonly the owner of the plate outlines and even details the elements of the design and the artist carries out the ideas as well as possible. Thus, in Dr. Ambrose M. Bailey's bookplate, the symbolism to be embodied was carefully thought out before the artist touched pen to paper. As the owner himself reads its meaning, it is as follows: "The lamp of learning with the books at the base, the lamp shedding an aureole upon 'For Christ and for Truth' superimposed upon a background of the cross of sacrifice and the circle of eternity, all throwing a light upon the open page." It is not always the case that the owner has so precise and detailed an idea of what he wants, but the artist is usually distinctly limited to carrying out the ideas of another person. Dr. Bailey's plate was the work of Miss Winifred Ward.

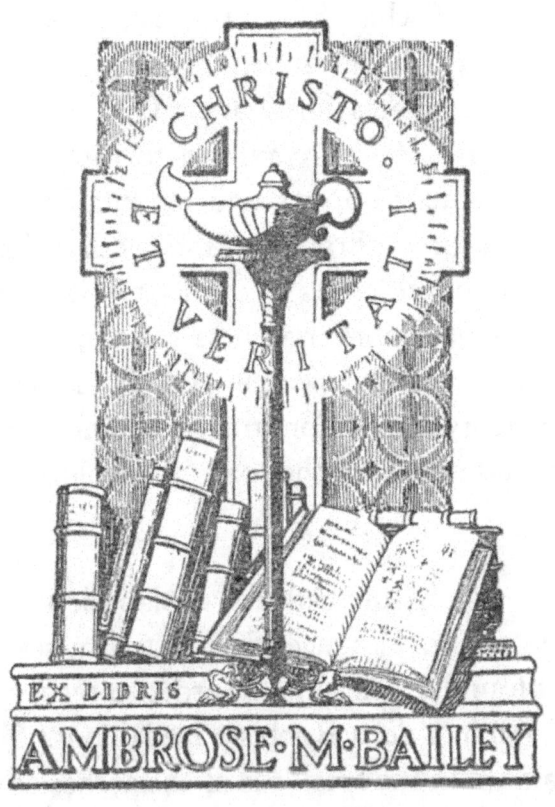

Rev. Ambrose M. Bailey's Plate
By Winifred Ward

Miss Jessie Fisken has designed a number of plates—ten of which are in our list. In subject they present a wide range, and in style much variety. Her plates for Francis G. Frink, Jr., and Spafford Frink are related to their fondness for outdoor sports and mountaineering. Her design for the Frances Skinner Edris Home is far from novel, either in itself or in its application, but its appropriateness for the institution is immediately evident and the lettering and accessory decoration are well combined to occupy and neatly fill the space available.

* * *

The design hardly calls for explanation. One need not go to Florence or to actually see its famous foundling hospital in order to recognize one of Andrea della Robbia's medallions. The originals are in the spandrils of the arches of its walls; they are in terra cotta, white against a blue ground. They are exquisitely done and evoke immediate sympathy. "At once humorous and pathetic", they present remarkable va-

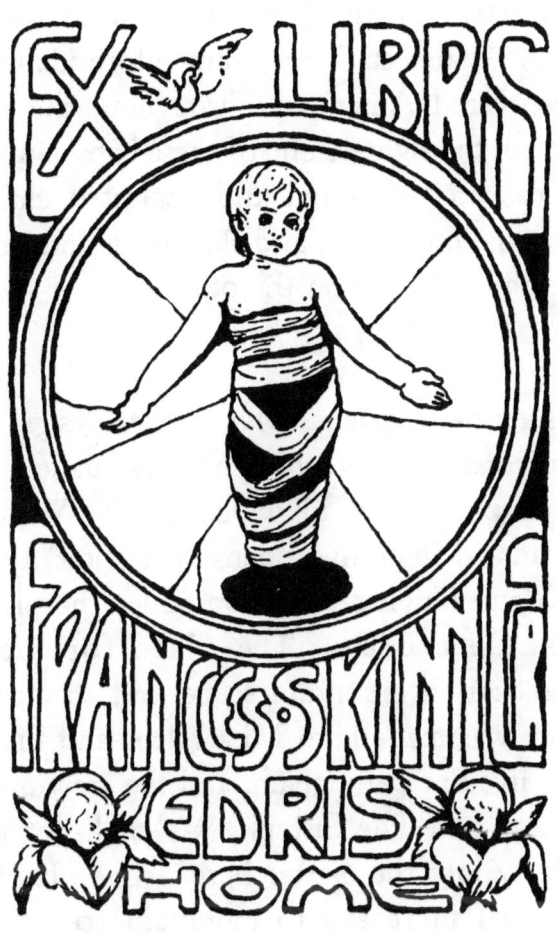

Bookplate of the Frances Skinner
Edris Home—By Jessie Fisken

riety, no two being alike. They were made about 1463, almost thirty years before Columbus discovered America. Throughout the entire world, the sight of one of these baby figures serves to recall deserted and neglected childhood on the one hand, and sheltering and protective philanthropy on the other.

* * *

Miss Annette Edens, who teaches design in the University of Washington, has made but four bookplates, two of which are for Washingtonians—Miss Olive Edens (her sister) and Prof. Glenn Hughes. We reproduce the plate of Miss Olive Edens. The plate for Prof. Hughes bears a mountain scene. At the time the plate was made both Miss Edens and Prof. Hughes lived in Bellingham, and the view is of Mt. Baker and The Sisters. We shall not go more fully into the matter here, as we plan to say a word in regard to mountain scenes as bookplate designs in a later article. So far as Miss Edens' Washington bookplates (we have not seen her others) are concerned, they are notable for the strength and simplicity of their designs. They gain much also in the printing. The Hughes plate is printed in gray; while the Olive Edens plate is printed in black, it has a delicate effect that is particularly pleasing.

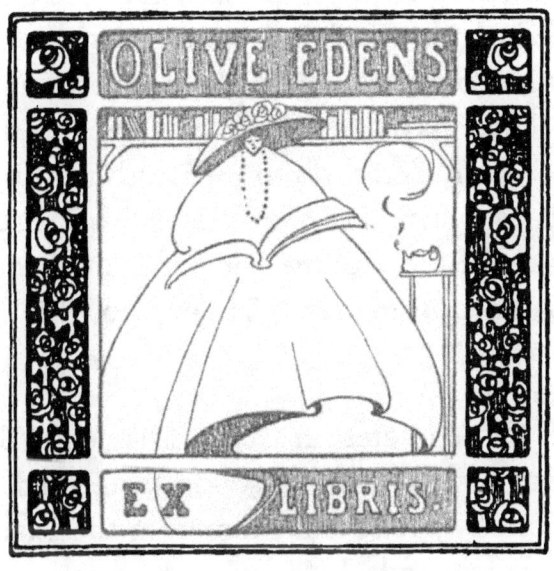

Miss Olive Edens' Bookplate
By Annette Edens

Prof. Edward Godfrey Cox, of the University of Washington, is not a professional artist, but a teacher in the Department of English. He has designed a number of bookplates and has a fondness for Irish designs. His own bookplate draws its motifs from the Book of Kells. One must look a little to make out the words Ex Libris, Edward Cox. At the bottom of the plate is a line in Irish, which is "a conventional scribal petition often found at the end of manuscript, 'God have mercy on the man of this book.'" Prof. Cox has also used Irish motifs in bookplates which he has designed for Prof. Chittick of Reed College and for Prof. Padelford of the University of Washington.

* * *

Prof. Cox's interest in Celtic ornamental designs was first aroused by seeing them used in woodwork by the school children in the Island of Tyree, Scotland. Later, when he came upon the Book of Kells, he was "deeply fascinated with the intricacy, delicacy, grotesqueness and adaptability of the motifs, as well as their end-less variation. Whatever the Irish borrowed, whether from Byzantine or Scandinavian, they turned into something peculiarly their own. They shook the symbolism out of the most tradi-tional of symbols, such as that of the four evan-gelists, and made them purely ornamental. The most characteristic are the interlacings and the diagonal fretting, which they borrowed from the Greeks. Their most original design is the grouped spirals." Prof. Cox has spent several summers in Ireland and Scotland, studying the Gaelic languages and literatures, both ancient and modern. He has accumulated a consider-able library in that especial field of research and is one of a group of scholars, who are collabor-ating in the collection of glossaries for an Old Irish dictionary.

* * *

What more remarkable source for illumina-tion designs is there than this same Book of Kells The choicest existing example of early Celtic illuminated manuscripts, it has outlasted

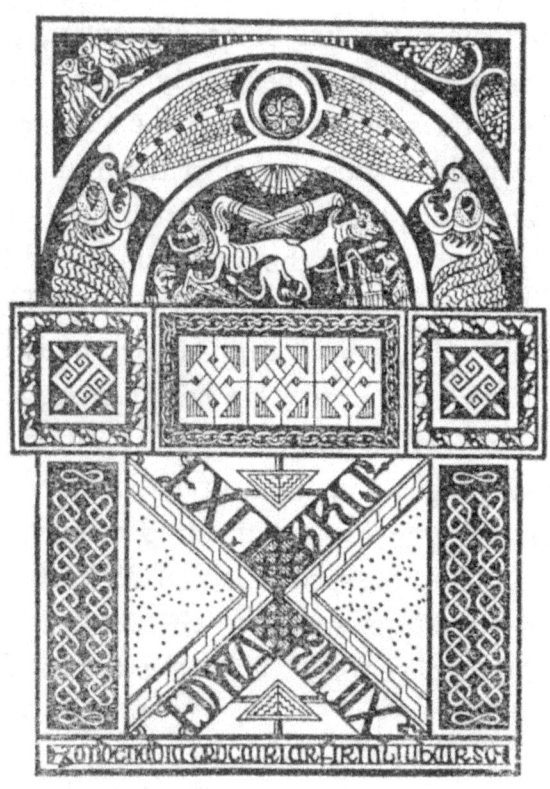

Plate of Edward Godfrey Cox
His Own Design

more than a thousand years. No one knows its actual date; it has been variously assigned to some time between the early sixth and the late ninth century. It has suffered from time and vandalism; the golden decoration of its covers has been stripped off; its vellum is stained from its concealment in a heap of filth; its colors are affected by age, but it remains a marvel of that patient, conscientious, time-consuming art, which was one of the glories of ancient Ireland. Of it Sullivan says: "Its weird and commanding beauty; its subdued and goldless coloring; the baffling intricacy of its fearless designs; the clean, unwavering sweep of rounded spiral; the creeping undulations of serpentine forms, that writhe in artistic profusion through the mazes of its decorations; the strong and legible minuscules of its text; the quaintness of its striking portraiture; the unwearied reverence and patient labor that brought it into being; all of which combined go to make up the Book of Kells, have raised this ancient Irish volume to a position of abiding eminence amongst the illuminated manuscripts of the world."

*   *   *

Prof. Westwood, who ought to know, considers its "monogram page"—"the most elaborate specimen of calligraphy which was perhaps ever executed." Its text lettering is fine and strong; its hundreds of initial letters are marvels of beauty and painstaking care and there is no repetition—no two of them are alike. As indicative of the enormous numbers of decorative elements it offers, there are more than a dozen in Prof. Cox's bookplate design.

*   *   *

Just after our first article was turned in, we saw the announcement that the Exhibition of the American Bookplate Society was to be in Seattle during November in connection with the Book Mart at Frederick & Nelson's. It gave our readers a chance to see something of what is going on in the bookplate world. As a matter of record, we make a few comments. The exhibition was the tenth annual display made by the society. It consisted of two hundred and five plates by seventy-one artists. Only designs completed during 1924 were eligible for entry. It was first shown at the National Arts Club in New York City—then at a number of cities through the United States. The exhibition was international and designs were displayed from England, Scotland, Canada, Australia, Sweden, Belgium, the United States — and, perhaps, other countries. Two classes of certificates were awarded—Merit, and Honorable Mention, four of each being given for different kinds of designs. The four certificates of merit were given to Roy Davis of Sydney, Australia (personal), Sidney Hunt of London, England (heraldic), Margaret Ely Webb of Santa Barbara, California (child) and Harriet Lundstrom of Stockholm, Sweden (institutional). Australia was unusually well represented and one certificate of merit and two certificates of honorable mention were awarded to Australians. One Washington artist was represented, Mr. George W.

Fuller of Spokane. Ought not this exhibition to come to Seattle every year? There is as much reason why it should be an annual event here as at other cities. By the way, we have at least two members of the American Bookplate Society in this state—Mr. Fuller of Spokane and Mrs. John W. Roberts (Olive W.) of Seattle.

III

UR second article was devoted to a group of Seattle artists who have designed bookplates. Information regarding the work of Mr. S. Gano Fotheringham came to hand too late to be included. Yet it is probable that Mr. Fotheringham has designed more bookplates than any artist therein considered. A list of thirteen designs is to his credit. Most of them suggest or represent the occupation or interests of the owners of the bookplates. The artist often shows much cleverness in combining elements that are not naturally associated. Thus in his plate for Ralph Day Major, he happily brings together devotion to legal study and fondness

for music. His flutter of musical notes is suggestive of the falling of autumnal leaves and
the drifting of petals of cherry blossoms in the
Japanese springtime. In Dr. E. Weldon Young's
plate he successfully groups Scotch tartan,
thistles, weapons and the warcry of the family
tradition.

* * *

In the plate by him we reproduce, that of Mr.
H. C. Henry, we have extreme simplicity rather
than ingenious grouping. The artists's part is
here really reduced to a minimum as he had
had to work from a direct photograph of the
object represented. From what a range of subjects, the owner had to make his choice! He
might have selected for his bookplate something
suggestive of his notable engineering achieve-
ments; he might have reminded himself of his
assistance to the needy children of France in an
hour of desperation. He has, however, selected
the entrance to his private art gallery for the
subject—simple, beautiful, and indicative of the

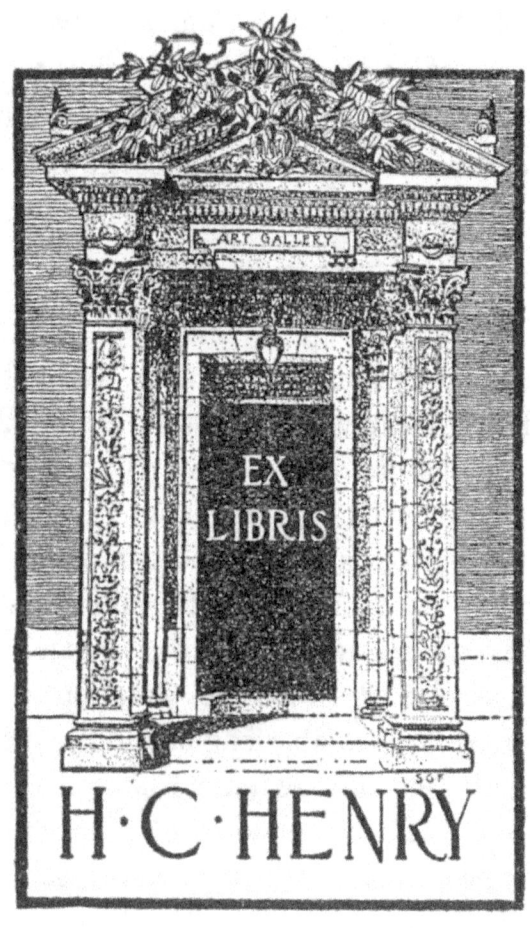

Bookplate of Mr. H. C. Henry

occupations and interests of the leisure hours in a busy life.

* * *

Among those who, in Seattle, have designed bookplates is Roi Partridge. He has left us for other fields, but his memory remains and several Washington bookplates must be credited to him. We have already mentioned how some professional artists look upon the making of bookplates. Mr. Partridge so thoroughly represents this attitude, that, in answer to a request for a list of his Washington bookplate designs, he wrote: "I am not interested in bookplates, I don't like to make them, don't want to be connected with them by reputation or otherwise. I think Gordon Craig aptly summed up the value of the exhibits in the title of his book, Nothing, or the Bookplate."

* * *

Among his designs is that for Mr. Charles E. Shepard. It is a piece of work, so delicately and conscientiously performed, that Mr. Partridge is hardly justified in cutting it adrift. It is pleas-

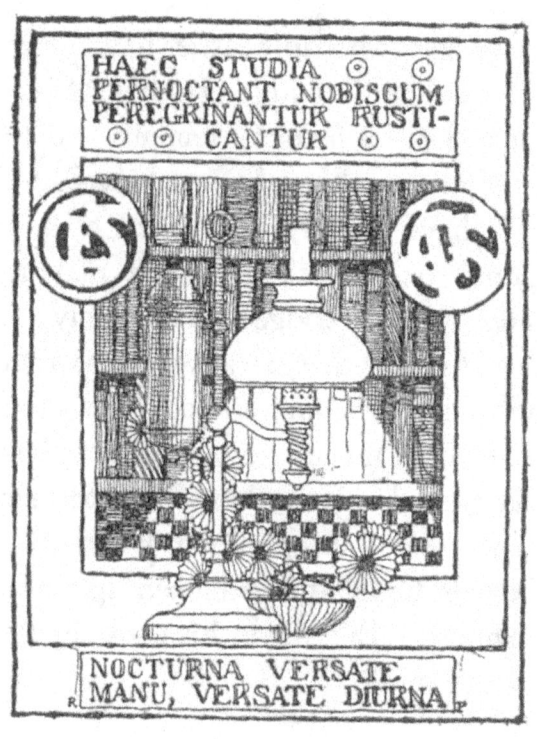

Bookplate of Mr. Charles E. Shepard

antly suggestive of scholarly tastes and quiet home joys. The well-filled shelves, the student lamp, the spray of flowers betray the tastes of the owner. Mr. Shepard himself translates the Latin mottoes. The upper one is from Cicero's oration in defence of the poet Archias and says: "These literary studies spend the nights with us, go down into country with us." The lower one is from Horace and says: "Turn them (books) over with your nightly and daily hands." The plate is an attractive piece of etching.

* * *

It is not our purpose here to go into a discussion of whether the bookplate is worth while, or to make a defence of the pastime of collecting and studying them. The matter has been much and bitterly discussed, pro and con. There are those who speak much worse of the ex libris than Roi Partridge. There are book-owners who aver that they "would be ashamed to spoil a valuable and prized volume by sticking a penny stamp in it." As to the collector of bookplates, hard things are said of him. His fad "is more puerile than the collecting of postage stamps" —"it is on a par with making a button-string." The defence against such slurs has been ably made by others. We take matters as they stand. We are only interested at present in the book-plates of Washington, their owners and their artists.

* * *

Writers about bookplates and collectors have worked out a sort of classification. Two main groups are recognized — armorial or heraldic, and pictorial. The earliest bookplates were German and appeared about 1450. For more than three hundred years most bookplates—German, French, English, and others — were armorial, bearing family or individual coats of arms. Thousands of armorial plates are known to collectors. Many of them are handsome and well executed, but a knowledge of heraldry is necessary, for their understanding. The careful study of the armorial bookplates of any given nation shows variation in treatment and style, in the course of time. Thus English armorials, which have been thoroughly studied, are divided into five classes — early armorials, Jacobean, Chippendale, ribbon and wreath, modern armorials. The early armorials were simple and without distinctive treatment. The Jacobean was heavily and symmetrically ornamental and prevailed from 1700 to about 1750. The Chippendale was lighter, more fanciful, and unbalanced; it came into vogue about 1750. The ribbon and wreath was a reaction against the heaviness of the one and the extreme ornateness of the others, but was in favor only for a score of years—from 1750 to 1770. Since it there has been no single well-marked armorial type in England. Modern armorials in that country show great diversity and have been influenced by all the types that have gone before.

* * *

Heraldic plates are, naturally, not common in the United States. Those that occur are those of foreigners who have lately cast in their lot with us or those of old families, who have—or think they have—a family coat-of-arms, which they are entitled to use. These last face difficulties. Heraldry is a precise and exacting science. Most Americans know nothing of it and are incompetent to decide whether they have a coat-of-arms or not. Ludicrous mistakes are made and most Americans will be wise to make use of a coat-of-arms — in bookplate or elsewhere—only after a careful investigation by an expert into their claims. Here in Washington we have many residents, some citizens, who have come from England or Canada and who have armorial rights and knowledge. Among them are some with bookplates, as the Rev. Leighton Howard-Smith and Daniel Caldwell Millett.

* * *

The other general class, showing immense diversity, is that of pictorials. Attempts to subdivide these sharply into groups or classes, regularly break down. There are, however, several groups, to which simple descriptive names are given, which need only to be mentioned to be understood. Thus, we speak of portrait, library interior, bookshelf or bookpile, landscape, symbolical, monogram, seal, bookplates. Such are immediately recognizable. Altogether in a class by themselves are what are commonly called rebus bookplates, where the design is in some sense or other a play upon the owners' name.

* * *

Of true rebus plates there are but few. Among heraldic plates are many instances of canting arms. Thus, an actual drake may figure in the coat-of-arms of one Drake, or a Moor's head occurs in the arms of a Moore. Usually, in such cases, there is some historic incident or some family tradition that explains the association. Whitman College uses a bookplate for the Myron Eels Collection of books in its library. It bears the Eels coat-of-arms, in which three eels occur, giving an example of canting arms. Another type of so-called rebus bookplates is found in non-armorials, where a simple word play on the name occurs in the pictorial design. Thus, a Kansas bookplate for some children named Beach shows the picture of a beach; one for a boy named Key shows a key. There are Washington bookplates of this kind. That of Dr. Alexander Hamilton Pea-cock, by Gano Fotheringham, uses peacocks, plumes, plume-eyes and pinnae, ingeniously combined, in a well-balanced and harmonious design. In a true rebus plate, however, the pic-torial elements would give syllabic sounds, which would have to be combined to give the name—and the picture elements would have no reference to the meaning of the name. I know of no true rebus bookplate in this State.

IV

WE planned to devote this article to book-plates of social clubs, but find we have only three in our list. The leading clubs usually have something of a library and many of them have bookplates which are at-tractive and appropriate. The three Washing-ton club bookplates that we know are those of the Sunset Club, the Women's University Club, and the Rainier Club. The bookplate of the Sunset Club is a rather elaborate pictorial. It shows a sun setting in the sea; in the foreground to the left are trees and to the right a peacock standing on a column that rises from a balustrade. The bird looks seaward and his ocellated tail trails behind. The person who presented me a copy of this striking bookplate writes: "The choice of the peacock for the bookplate of the Sunset Club has been the subject of comment. I am inclined to think that this bird appears in the Club's bookplate, as it appears in the decorations of the Club, chiefly because it lends itself well to decoration. I would not like to have it thought that the silly bird is in any wise a club emblem." Surely no one could indulge in an uncharitable thought in such a matter.

*   *   *

The bookplate of the Women's University Club is less striking and decorative, but it seems to carry a bit of sentiment. Today the Club has its large and convenient building, made for its express use and developed with regard to work

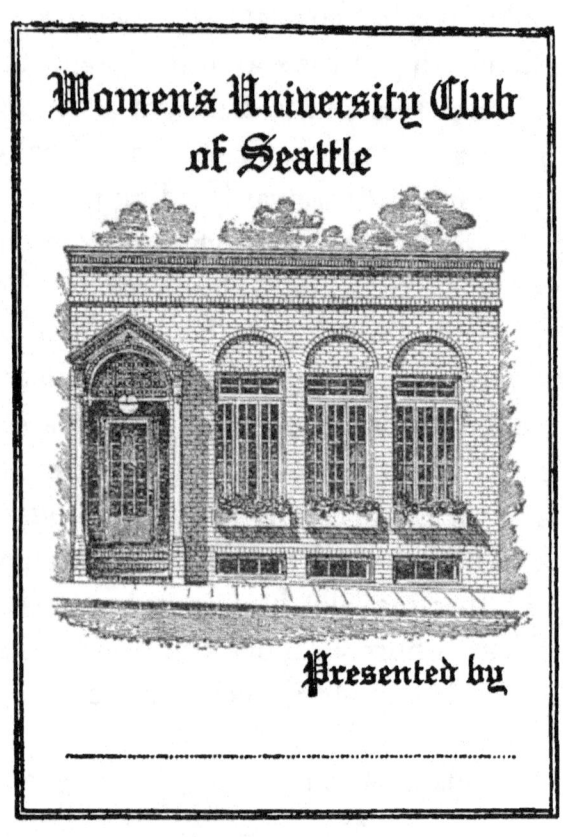

The Bookplate of the Women's
University Club.

in all the lines of its various departments and interests. Its bookplate harks back to the older, simpler days. The design of the plate is a representation of their old quarters, a reminder of the days of "auld lang syne."

* * *

The Rainier Club's bookplate belongs to the group of portrait bookplates. It is a bold and handsome plate bearing as central design the reproduction of an oil painting of Peter Rainier, Admiral of the Blue, which is still preserved in England. It is not for me, a newcomer to Seattle, to attempt to inform Washingtonians concerning the man for whom their most splendid mountain is named. When Vancouver saw its rounded, snow-capped mass on May 7, 1792, he said: ' . . . after my friend, Rear Admiral Rainier, I distinguished it by the name of Mount Rainier." (The name was spelled Regnier formerly.) The portrait here used as a design, must have been painted about 1805, as it was in that year that Rear Admiral (and Vice Admiral) Rainier became "Admiral of the

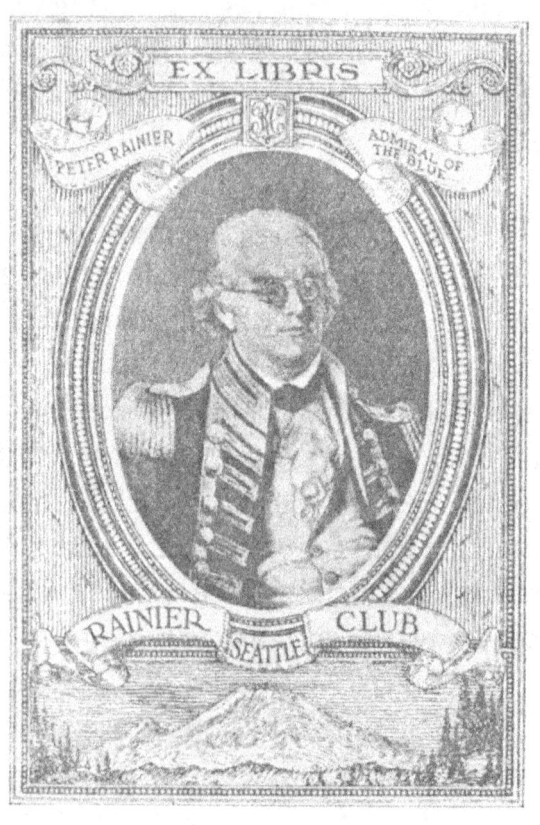

EX LIBRIS

PETER RAINIER   ADMIRAL OF THE BLUE

RAINIER   SEATTLE   CLUB

The Rainier Club's Bookplate

Blue." He died three years later, in 1808. Below the portrait, in the bookplate, is a general view of the mountain that was "distinguished" by the naming. The grouping of the different pictorial elements and wording makes an effective and attractive plate.

As a rule portrait plates are not a great success. That of the Rainier Club is good because of the boldness of the portrait, the uniform, and the framing, which give a medallion effect. Two portrait plates, well known to collectors and making a satisfactory impression, are the bookplates of the John Crerar library (Chicago), and the American Antiquarian Society (Worcester, Mass.). They are the work of bookplate artists of national, even international, reputation. That the plate of the Rainier Club deserves mention in connection with them, is really high praise. There are not many portrait ex-libris in our Washington collection. Two of them, however, are of exceptional interest and in both the treatment is happy. They are the bookplates of Wayne Albee (by Allen Clark) and M. Ross Downs. Mr. Albee's plate presents a likeness of the owner neatly brought into relation with the equipment of that craft, through the exercise of which the owner has given so much of delight to the readers of The Town Crier and the citizens of Seattle in general. Mr. Downs' plate represents him as seated on the very tip of the extreme summit of Denny Peak, near Snoqualmie Pass. It is a reproduction process plate, made from a photograph taken by Mr. Thomas J. Acheson. The originality of idea in both these plates, and the excellence of its working out, put them far above the usual bookplates of the portrait class.

*　*　*

That a considerable number of the landscape bookplates of Washington should represent mountains is natural enough. Mountain designs are not, however, uncommon, elsewhere. Thus, Japan's peerless Fuji is the design in many bookplates — not only for Japanese but for others also. George W. Eve, the famous British engraver of ex-libris, rarely goes outside of heraldic designs, in which he is the absolute master, but he has made one splendid Mount Fuji book-plate. J. W. Spenceley was, in his time, the most famous designer of landscape bookplates in America. The most elaborate bookplate he ever made, perhaps, was one for a collection of books regarding Mexico, in which the central element of the design was Popocatepetl—"much smoking mountain." Here in Washington we have a choice of mountain scenery and there is no dearth of beautiful subjects. We do not know just what mountains are represented in the book-plates of Miss Merrill and Spafford Frink. But, in the plate designed for Clifford Cole Corbet by George W. Fuller we have a fine mirror-view of Rainier; in Annette Eden's plate for Prof. Glenn Hughes an extremely simple repre-sentation of Mount Baker and the Sisters as seen from Bellingham, is remarkably satisfying; and this plate of Mr. Downs, introducing the tip of Denny Peak, gives a wild and barren sug-ren suggestion of difficulties surmounted that is extremely good. Speaking of clubs and of bookplates with mountain designs—have not The Mountaineers a library, and a bookplate to mark their volumes? It seems natural that they would have one—and it should be notable.

V

THIS article was set apart for the consideration of Institutional Bookplates—those of institutions of higher learning, public libraries, learned societies, etc. here too the bookplates of such charitable and benevolent institutions as hospitals, asylums, homes, etc., would be in place. As we approach the subject, we find ourselves in the situation of an ophidean quester in Erin. "There are no snakes in Ireland." So, we may almost say, "There are no institutional bookplates in Washington." Few indeed are the universities, colleges, public libraries, hospitals, asylums and "homes" that seem to feel the need of a real bookplate. The Frances Skinner Edris home has a pretty plate, to which we have already called attention. In Spokane, the Hutton Settlement has a good plate designed by Mr. Fuller. We have seen no other bookplates in this class.

* * *

As to public libraries, few in Washington have aught but a plain and simple "book-label," often of the ugliest. The State Library and the State Law Library at Olympia use a simple label. They have also a perforating stamp that perforates evidence of ownership in the very leaves of the book. The immediate and evident purpose of preventing theft is unquestionably achieved. Nothing more is absolutely necessary. The Seattle Public Library, one of the good libraries of the United States, shows no tendency to encourage art in this direction. It has a label for the books of the reference department, which can hardly be outdone in ugliness. It serves its purpose, but surely gives no feeling of pleasure or satisfaction to the user of the books. The only public library in the state, so far as we know, that has an attractive and artistic bookplate is the public library of Spokane. It is, of course,

Mr. Fuller's work. It is printed in black and green on a light green paper. It is intended to mark books presented to the library. Intertwining vines with fruit and foliage frame a space for the lettering and library symbol. It is a satisfying piece of work.

* * *

As to colleges and universities, little can be said. Most of them have simple labels, often printed from type. When I first asked the University of Washington for its bookplate, perhaps in 1914, it used a mere plain label, which was, however, a neat piece of work, the good taste of which partly redeemed the situation. Today the University uses a real bookplate, the design of which is probably the reproduction of its official seal. It then represents a recognized type of ex-libris, which we have not met before among the bookplates of the state. Whitman College uses for its general library a heraldic bookplate, which presumably reproduces the coat-of-arms of the Whitman family. It is far from beautiful.

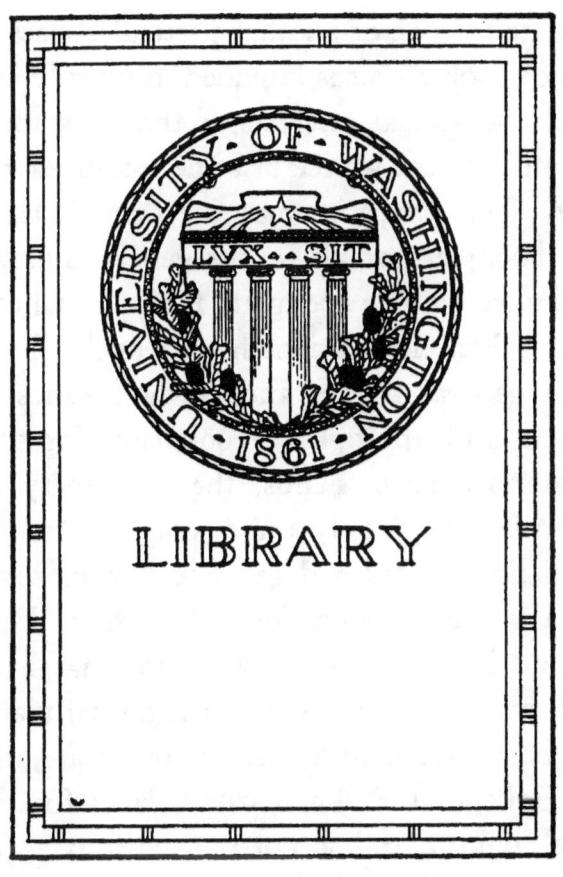

LIBRARY

The University of Washington Bookplate

Universities and colleges often use a special bookplate for one or another particular class or group of books. This is intended to sharply emphasize the special interests of the institution, or to indicate the source of some treasured collection. The institution may use a simple label, or no bookplate at all for its general library, but may have a fine bookplate for a special collection. Some institutions have a fine ex-libris for the general library and a whole series of beautiful and appropriate bookplates for subordinate divisions. Thus, the University of California has not only a fine bookplate for the general library, but a dozen fine designs serve for many special collections. Columbia, Harvard and Michigan are institutions that have gone heavily into the use of such special plates for subordinate collections. In our state, the State College at Pullman uses a label for the general library and a portrait bookplate for books bought through the Overman Memorial Fund. Whitman College, besides its regular bookplate, mentioned above, has a special plate

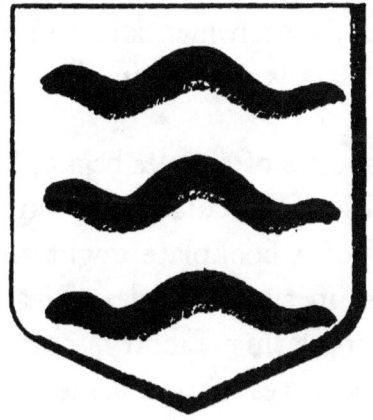

Bookplate of the Eels Northwest History Collection in the Library of Whitman College

for the Eels Northwest History Collection. It, too, is a heraldic bookplate,' reproducing the Eels family arms, dating from 1705. These are "canting arms," in the nature of rebus, and the plate has already been mentioned in an earlier article. The plate is printed in blue.

* * *

When this series of articles began, I had seen no bookplates of circulating libraries. The actual utility of a bookplate might seem to be at its greatest in such libraries. Hearing of a Bookplate Circulating Library, curiosity was aroused and an investigation made. Perhaps it was interested in encouraging collectors, by circulating information regarding ex-libris, or by aiding in the exchange of specimens? No such interest was found. The library was one of the usual sort, but it uses a real bookplate, a pictorial. Later it was found that the Sparrow's Nest Circulating Library has a bookplate, the design being a chirping sparrow. No doubt other circulating libraries use bookplates, but it is unlikely that they would be especially interesting or attractive, and most of them would no doubt be used as an "advertisement," either of the library itself or some of its side lines, as candy, picture postcards, etc.

* * *

I believe, too, that the bookplates of circulating libraries would often be "commercial" bookplates. These are the bane of the real lover of bookplates and the collector. Every now and again some business house—usually one that supplies bookcases and library furniture—gets out ten or a dozen little designs—not always lacking in artistic merit, but regularly lacking in meaning. These are without an owner's name. Through advertisement or correspondence, a book owner is led to send for a free sample set of these. In getting them, he supplies details regarding his library, which it is to the interest of the house to know. He is then given the opportunity to have his name printed on any plate, the design of which pleases him, at a ridiculously cheap price. Behold him now supplied with a bookplate, at a bargain. Of course, he has had no word in dictating the development of the design; none of his little conceits or fancies is embodied in it; Tom, Dick and Harry, anywhere and everywhere, may be using the same plate—only with their names in place of his. The commercial plate falls short artistically, and its design soon palls. As the user does not own the plate from which the prints were made, he is never sure of getting a new supply, when his original supply is exhausted. Whether bookplates are, or are not, worth while—their main claim to respect is the degree to which the personality of the owners enter into them. The working out of an idea; the imparting of a distinctive individuality to the design; the having of a bit of art work by a real artist for one's own use; satisfaction in technique, in paper, in printing; the feeling that a plate is one's own, unshared with others; these are the chief joys of ex-libris ownership. **And, none of these can possibly come from a** "commercial" bookplate.

VI

HE two things that most interest me in bookplates are the way in which they embody the ideals of their artists and the personality of their owners. The hint that they give of the taste, the fancies and the interests of their users is a delight. We have already called attention to some examples of this personality expression in a number of plates, which were introduced as specimens of the work of one or another artist. In this article we shall mention three plates into which this element of personality conspiciously enters. Prof. Edmond S. Meany's plate is far from beautiful but it has an interesting story. It shows three knives, differing in size and form. Above is Ex libris; below, Edmond S. Meany. Of this plate the owner says: "In my work on the biography of Chief Joseph Nez Perces, I had personal visits with him and during one of these he gave me the name of Three Knives, or in their own language, Metatwultz. He would not say why he gave me that name, but after his death his friends told me that many years before he had a friend among the younger leaders of the Sioux, who was tall and straight and was known by the name of Three Knives. That friend had died and he was complimenting me by transferring the name and keeping the reason for it to himself. A friendly printer, learning about this name, prepared the bookplate which I have gladly used ever since."

* * *

Another bookplate that interests me on account of the owner's personality is that of Rev. Herbert H. Gowen. It is printed in chocolate brown on a buff paper. It is, of course, Oriental in its suggestions. It "was designed by Mr. A. W. S. Lee of Anking, China, well known for his two volumes of translations from Chinese poetry. The main idea is that of life, rich in experience through the contemplation of the past—made visible and vocal in literature. The glory of the past, illumining all the path, is indicated by the rays of the setting sun."

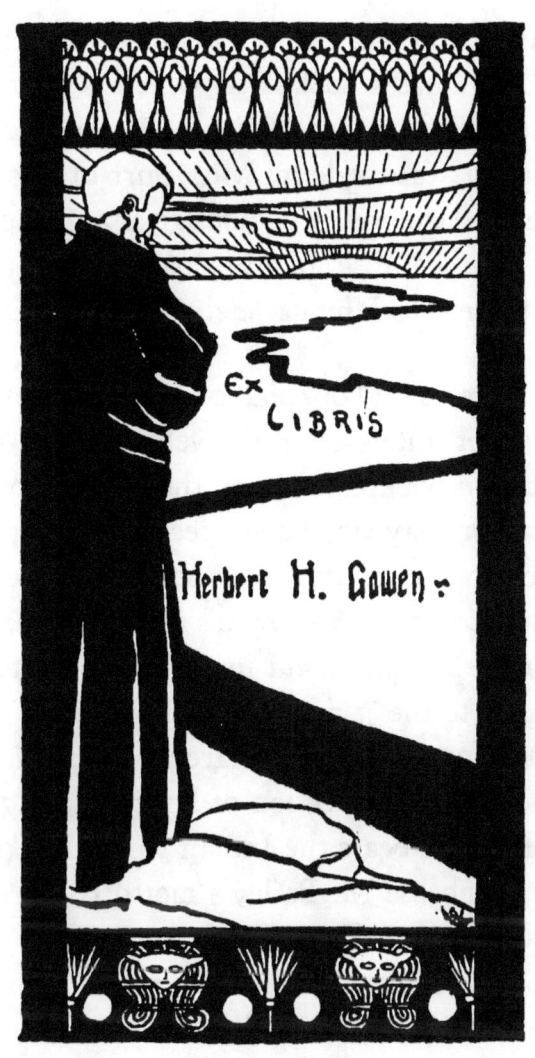

Bookplate of Rev. Herbert H. Gowen

President Stephen B. L. Penrose of Whitman College has a bookplate, which is remarkably satisfying in the quality of its art workmanship. It was made by Miss Burr of Boston and is a seal-armorial. The design is an adaptation of the Penrose family coat-of-arms and carries the motto *Ubique fidelis*—ever faithful.

* * *

The mottoes on bookplates are in themselves a matter of interest. Relatively few of the Washington bookplates carry them. Such mottoes may or may not have special and appropriate reference to books and bookish interests. Professor Louis F. Anderson's bookplate bears the words *epea pteroenta* in Greek characters. They refer to the "winged words," which literature has for its lovers. Clarence B. Bagley's bookplate for his collection of books relating to the Northwest, bears the Indian word, *An-kut-ty*. Dr. Ambrose M. Bailey's motto is *Christo et veritate*—"for Christ and for truth." In Prof. Clark P. Bissett's plate the motto appears as an inscription above a fireplace—"The race is not to the swift, nor the battle to the strong, but the victory is unto him who is faithful." Miss Adeline S. Cooke has a verse that refers to books:

> "Great friends and true
> In gallant train
> My treasure ships
> Bring o'er the main."

The design is attractive and the whole idea —picture and motto—is appropriate to a librarian. We have already mentioned the Irish scribal petition that occurs on Prof. Edward Godfrey Cox's plate, which translated reads, "God have mercy on the man of this book." Under the picture of Mr. M. Ross Downs on his rocky pinnacle we read: *Successus persever-antia*. Whether the success that comes through perseverence is the mere victory of the mountain climber, or whether it has a general reference to difficulties surmounted, or a special application to strength gained through mastery of books—the motto fits the design well. In his witches' caldron plate, which is calculated to make one's hair rise, Mr. George W. Fuller plainly does not mean to betray too easily his meaning in the words: *Emen hatan satute icy satute le jove icy jove la sabath.* It is best not to look too closely into matters connected with the witch sabbath. The motto, *Manus haec inimica tyrranis,* "this hand inimical to tyrants," is a part of the coat-of-arms in Daniel Caldwell Millett's plate. In Miss Mauda Margaret Polley's plate, which by the way was designed by Sidney Hunt, one of the favorite London bookplate artists, we read: "The dear and the dumpy twelves," which is bookish enough. The Latin mottoes on Mr. Charles E. Shepard's plate are admirably chosen and in full harmony with the idea of an ex-libris. Dr. Edward Lincoln Smith's beautiful bookplate bears the words: *Fides, Spes, Potestas*—faith, hope, power. Such are the mottoes of our Washington booplates.

* * *

Not uncommonly bookplates bear warnings to borrowers or book-thieves. We know but

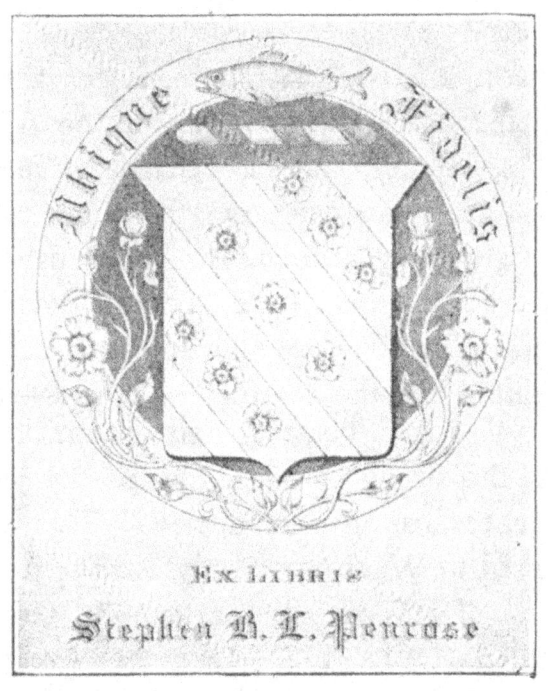

Dr. S. B. L. Penrose's Bookplate

one such in this state. Mr. Daniel S. Kinney uses a plain book^label which says: "And please return it. You may think this is a strange request, but I find that although many of my friends are poor mathematicians, they are near'ly all of them good book-keepers.—Scott."

Sometimes a bookplate is made to carry a special message. The fine one for the Allen-town Free Library, James L. Schaadt Memorial, carries such a message from the donor, with his autograph signature below. It reads: "A kindly heart—a quiet voice—polite words and manners—a hand open to help—attention to little things for the comfort of others—free-dom from anger, boasting and patronizing—toward the strong courage, toward the weak chivalry, toward all men fairness." This book is credited to Washington only because it was the work of a Washington artist, Mr. George W. Fuller.

* * *

Probably more medical men own and use bookplates than men of other professions. This conviction has grown gradually upon me, but I believe it to be a fact. And most physicians who have bookplates make them talk shop. One might easily bring together a gruesome series of skulls, crossbones, skeletons, instruments, etc. There are fewer physicians in our Washington list of bookplate owners than we expected. We know only Doctors Downs, Epplen, Peacock, Young and Veasey. Dr. Downs' plate is typical. A physician sits at a table on which are mortar, pestle, scales, retort, etc.; he is making a test, and holds the test-tube up to the light to observe the reaction; behind him a skeleton peers at the test-tube, while a black cat rubs herself against the doctor's leg. In Dr. Epplen's plate we have the centaur, Chiron, and the young Asclepius, whose staff with twining snakes betrays his identity and craft. In Dr. Veasey's plate it is Hygeia who has the caduceus and despatches healing on the breezes.

*   *   *

As we write these words we learn that Mr. Fuller's A Bibliography of Bookplate Literature is just off the press. Published by the Spokane Public Library, it is a beautiful piece of work which does honor to our state. Its preparation has been an arduous task. Mr. Fuller is the editor and supplies a forword. Mrs. Vera B. Grimm of the Spokane Library force has done the bibliographical work. Mr. Winward Prescott of Boston, one of the best men in the bookplate field, has contributed "some random thoughts on bookplate literature." Paper, printing and binding are all of the best and the three who have shared in the work are to be congratulated upon the result. Periodical articles on bookplates, which are immensely numerous and practically inaccessible, are not listed. The work enumerates and characterizes about 800 books and brochures devoted to bookplates and lists some seventy other books which contain important ex-libris material. Were we not right in saying there is a veritable library of bookplate writings?

* * *

What we say above regarding medical bookplates seems to be borne out by the Bibliography. There are nine books or brochures that are devoted to the bookplates of physicians. These are in English, French and Bohemian. Cosgrove has written on Irish bookplates of doctors. Curtin's brochure on the bookplates of American physicians is well known and exceptionally interesting. Olivier has written a causerie upon his collection of the bookplates of French physicians and pharmacists of the past. Why should doctors, of all professionals, be more addicted to the use of bookplates? We do not attempt to answer the question.

* * *

In the first of these articles we stated our desire to make a list of bookplate owners in the State of Washington; to call attention to some plates of special interest; to describe some that were notable from the personality of their owners, for their significance, or their fitness; to make known the work of our artists in this field. To some degree, we have attained these ends. They have been imperfectly achieved. We have carried the list of known Washington bookplates to 150. It is but a beginning. No doubt many remain unmentioned, which equal in artistic merit and interest any of those we have described.

List of Washington Bookplates

Unless otherwise credited, these represent Seattle

Adams, Joseph Quincy, Ithaca, N. Y.
Albee, Wayne.
Allen, Edward W.
Allentown Free Library, Allentown, Pa.
Ames, Edgar.
Ames, Henry Semple, St. Louis, Mo.
Anderson, Louis F., Walla Walla.
Bagley, Clarence B.
Bailey, Ambrose M.
Ballou, C. C., Spokane.
Bissett, Clark Prescott.
Bloedel, Charlotte (2 varieties).
Blum, John Ralph.
Bookplate Circulating Library.
Brand, Cecil.
Brown, Annie M.
Chickering, Katherine, Spokane.
Chittich, Victor Lovitt Oakes, Portland, Ore.
College Club.
Comer, William D.
Conklin, Robert H.
Cooke, S. Adelina, Pullman.
Corbet, Clifford Cole, Spokane.

Corbet, Jr., James McCrea, Spokane.
Cox, Edward Godfrey.
Davenport, Jr., Lewis M., Spokane.
Diem, Eugenia.
Dodge, Alice.
Donovan, Jr., William.
Dowling, Grace.
Downs, George A., Spokane.
Downs, M. Ross.
Easson, Graeme Sanford, Spokane.
Edens, Olive, Bellingham.
Edris Home, Frances Skinner.
Epplen, Frederick, Spokane.
Epplen, Maria Dorothea, Spokane.
Farnham, William Horatio, Spokane.
Fisken.
Foote, William W., Pullman.
Freeman, Helen, Pasadena, Cal.
Friedlander, Leon A.
Frink, Jr., Francis G.
Frink, Spafford.
Fuller, George W., Spokane (3 designs).
Fursman, Eleanor, Cordova, Alaska.
Gailey, Walter R.
Genevieve (Fuller), Spokane.
Gowen, Herbert H.
Graves, William G., Spokane.
Green, Hortense.

Harding, George Laban, Tacoma.
Harper, Paul Coates.
Henry, H. C.
Howard-Smith, Leighton.
Hughes, Glenn.
Hughes, Mrs. Glenn.
Hull, Frank Wilton.
Hutton Settlement Library, Spokane.
James, Mrs. Burton.
Jencks (Gailey), Zalia.
Jennings, Eleanor.
Jensen, Martha.
Kapak, Louis, Spokane.
Kelleher, Daniel and Elise.
Kinney, Daniel S.
Kinney, Jessie Banks.
Lear, Harry B.
Leuthold, John Heitman, Spokane.
Linden, Adolph F.
Lovejoy, Albert R.
Lyman, Harold William.
Major, Ralph Day.
MacDonald, Helen.
Maxwell, Ora L., Spokane.
May, Mary Josephine.
Meany, Edmond S.
Medley, Edward F., Cordova, Alaska.
Merrill, Eulalie.

Merrill, Virginia.
Millet, Daniel Caldwell, Chehalis.
Morgan, R. E.
Old National Bank, Spokane.
Ostrander, H. F.
Padelford, Frederick Morgan.
Peacock, Alexander Hamilton.
Penrose, S. B. L., Walla Walla.
Perry, Jeannette.
Phillips, Mrs. George, Spokane.
Polley, Mauda Margaret, Chehalis.
Price, Jessie Easson, Spokane.
Prosch, Thomas W.
Prosser, Genevieve and William.
Puget Sound, College of, Tacoma (2 labels).
Rainier Club.
Roberts, Dorothy.
Roberts, Marinda.
Roberts, Olive W.
Rollins, Alice W.
Seattle Public Library.
Shepard, Charles E.
Sherwin, Parker, Spokane.
Smith, Edward Lincoln.
Smith, Gladys, Spokane.
Sparrow's Nest Circulating Library.
Spokane Masonic Library, Spokane.
Spokane Public Library, Spokane.

State College of Washington, Pullman
(2 designs).

Stevens, Marjorie.

Stone, George F.

Sunset Club.

Suzzallo, Henry.

Tatsch, Jacob Hugo, Cedar Rapids, Iowa.
(2 designs).

Termaat, M. Inez, New York City.

Thompson, Thomas Gordon.

Todd, Lucy.

University of Washington. (2 designs and label).

Veasey, Clarence Archibald, Spokane.

Vincent, W. D., Spokane.

Washington State Library, Olympia (label).

Weissbrodt, Irwin A.

Whites, The.

Whitman College, Walla Walla. (2 designs).

Wilson, John and Mary.

Wilson, Kathryn S.

Wilson, Will D.

Women's University Club.

Wood, James A..

Young, Betty.

Young, E. Weldon.

Young, M. Harwood.

Ziegler, Winfred H., Elgin, Ill.